T0065212

Quotes
From
The Future

Quotes

From

The Future

LANCE OWEN

QUOTES FROM THE FUTURE

iUniverse books may be ordered through booksellers or by contacting:

iUniverse
1663 Liberty Drive
Bloomington, IN 47403
www.iuniverse.com
844-349-9409

ISBN: 978-1-6632-1078-4 (sc)
ISBN: 978-1-6632-1079-1 (e)

Library of Congress Control Number: 2020920032

Print information available on the last page.

iUniverse rev. date: 12/16/2020

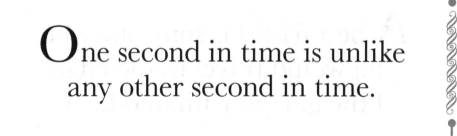

One second in time is unlike
any other second in time.

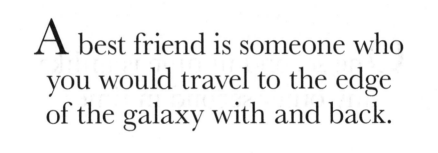

A best friend is someone who you would travel to the edge of the galaxy with and back.

All of the colors were together in harmony at the big bang.

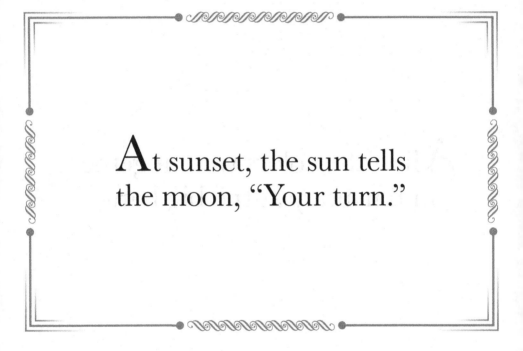

At sunset, the sun tells the moon, "Your turn."

Be fearless with what you post online.

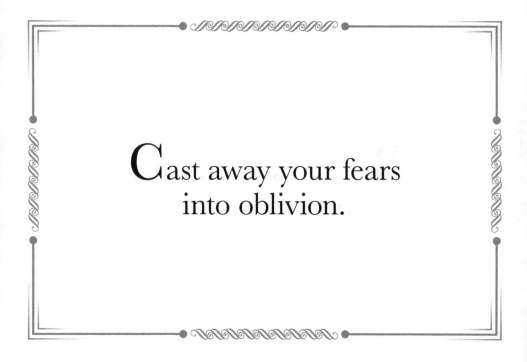

Cast away your fears
into oblivion.

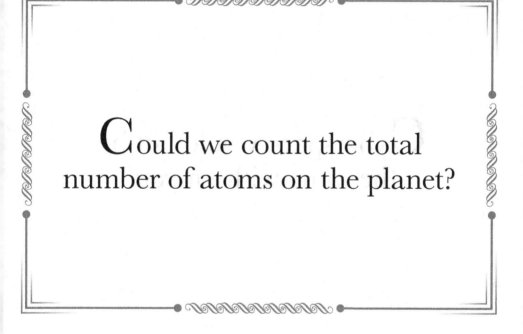

Could we count the total number of atoms on the planet?

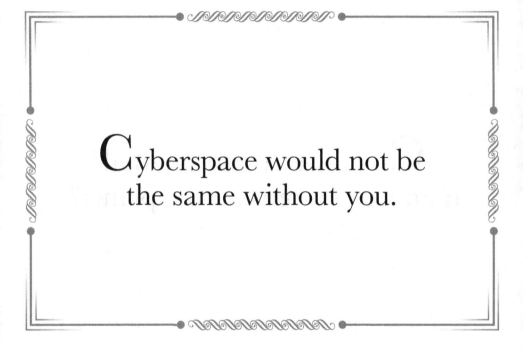

Cyberspace would not be the same without you.

Delete obsolete contacts,
but save your elite contacts.

Delete offbeat comments,
but save upbeat comments.

Elite contacts are those with the best ideas.

Endless designs that we
could create exist.

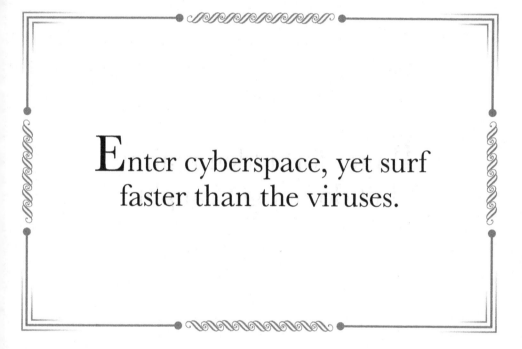

Enter cyberspace, yet surf faster than the viruses.

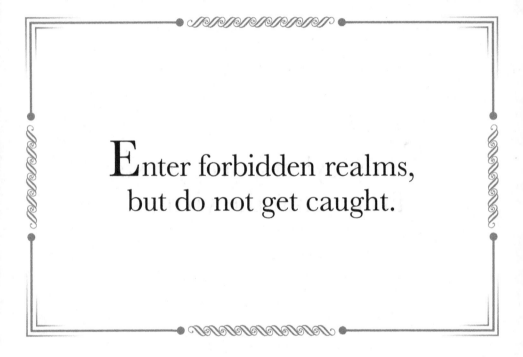

Enter forbidden realms,
but do not get caught.

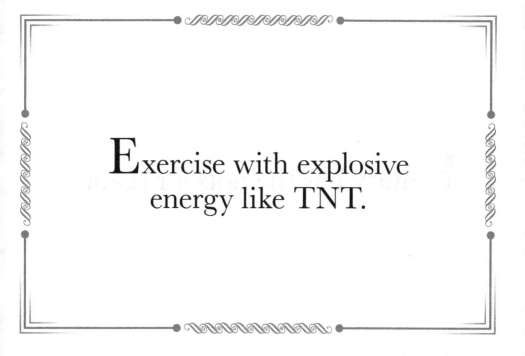

Exercise with explosive
energy like TNT.

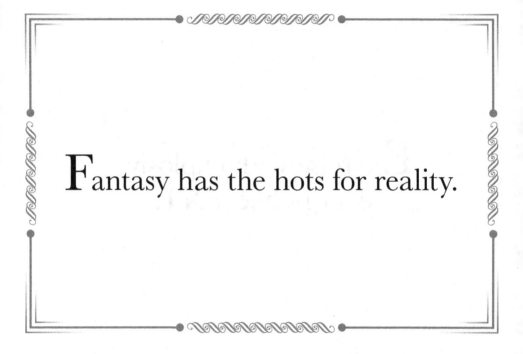

Fantasy has the hots for reality.

Feel at home anywhere
in the world.

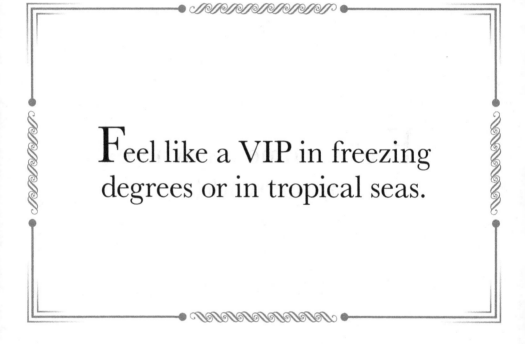

Feel like a VIP in freezing degrees or in tropical seas.

Feel the freshest you
have ever felt.

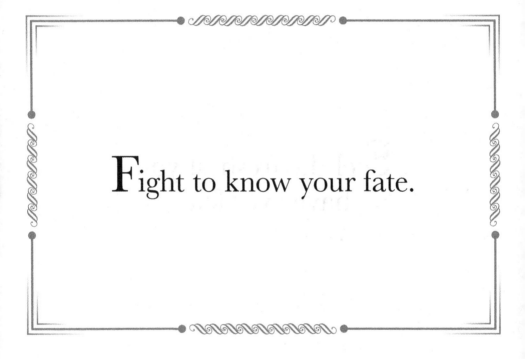

Fight to know your fate.

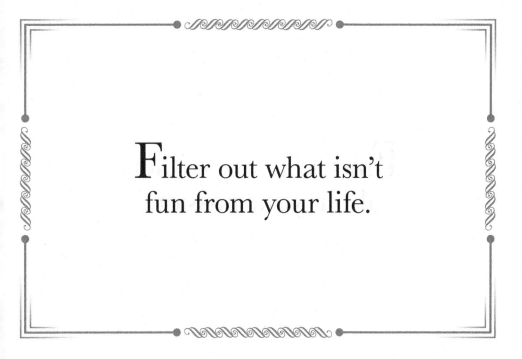

Filter out what isn't
fun from your life.

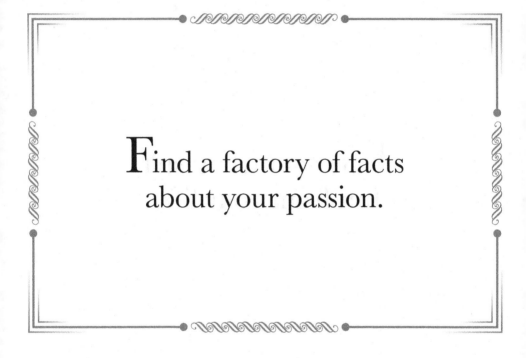

Find a factory of facts
about your passion.

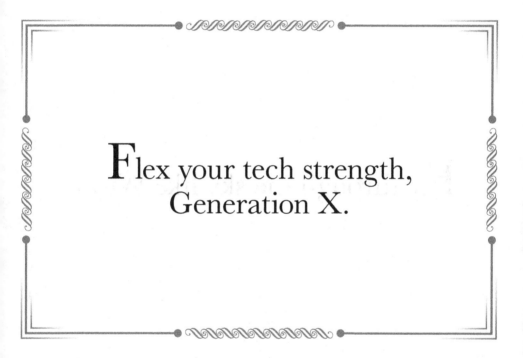

Flex your tech strength,
Generation X.

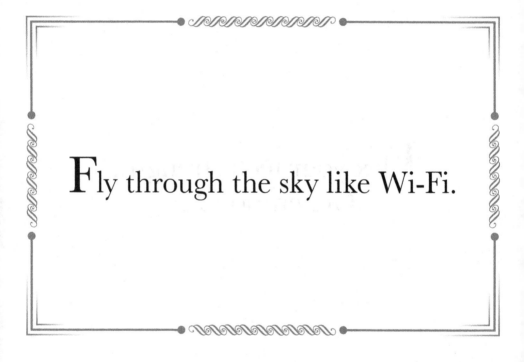

Fly through the sky like Wi-Fi.

Formulate the rate
to your own fate.

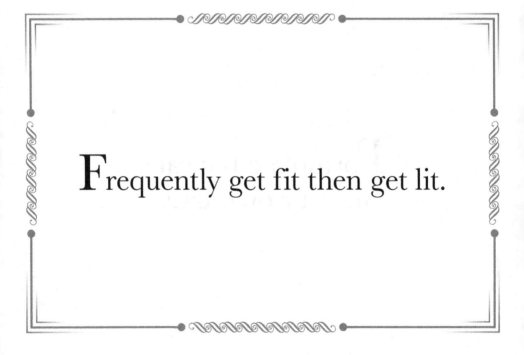

Frequently get fit then get lit.

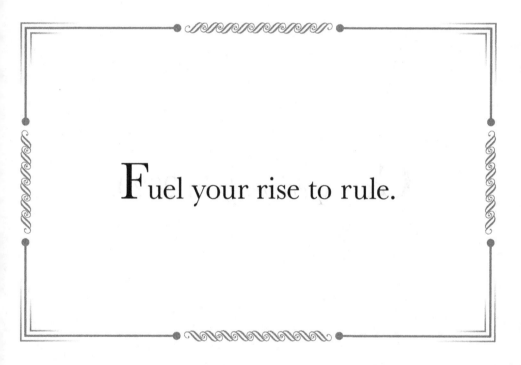

Fuel your rise to rule.

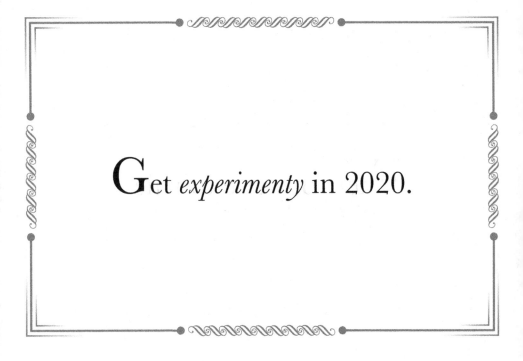

Get *experimenty* in 2020.

God could not have done a better job creating this planet.

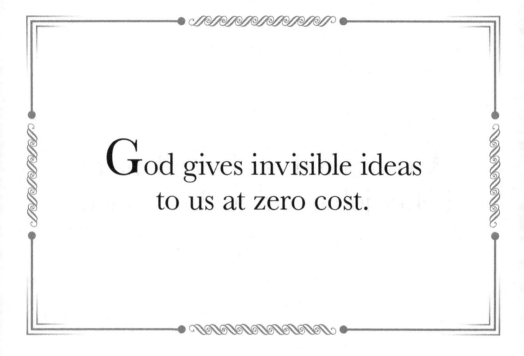

God gives invisible ideas
to us at zero cost.

I am a *kidult*!

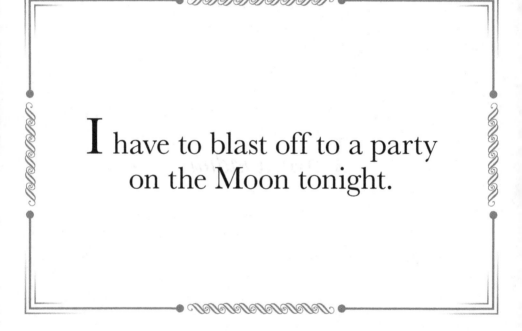

I have to blast off to a party
on the Moon tonight.

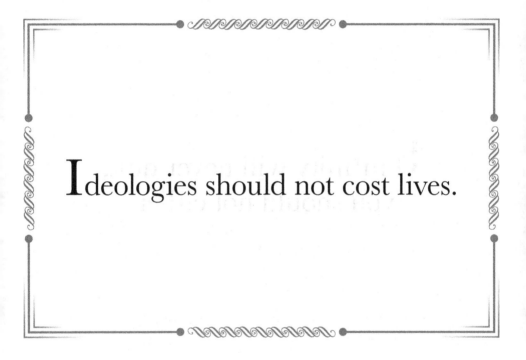

Ideologies should not cost lives.

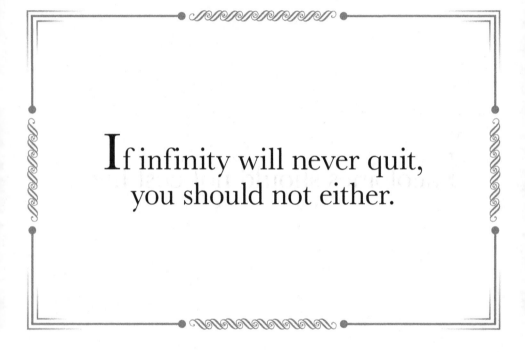

If infinity will never quit,
you should not either.

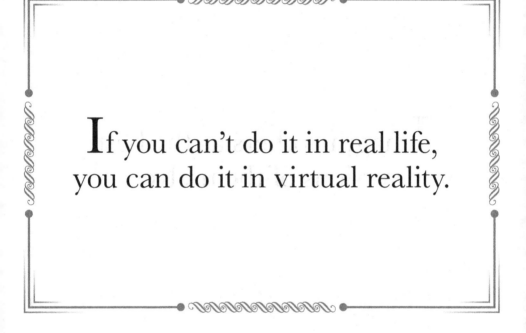

If you can't do it in real life,
you can do it in virtual reality.

Imagine others as the best
versions of themselves.

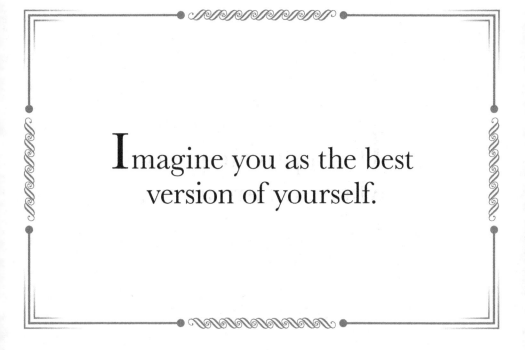

Imagine you as the best
version of yourself.

It is a private party
when you are alone.

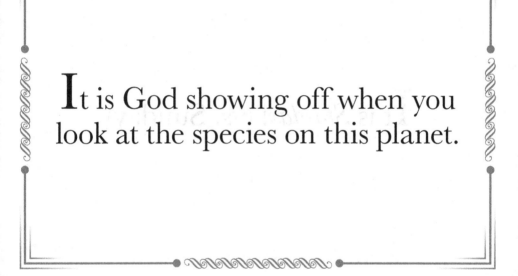

It is God showing off when you look at the species on this planet.

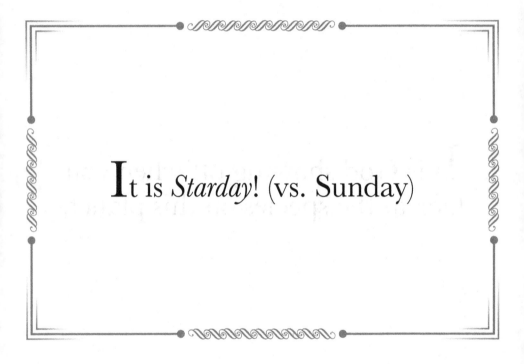

It is *Starday*! (vs. Sunday)

It is the best time to make
the biggest splash.

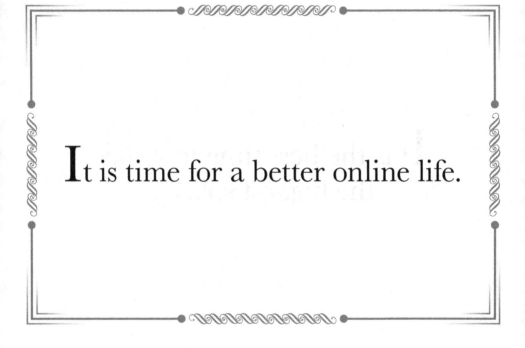

It is time for a better online life.

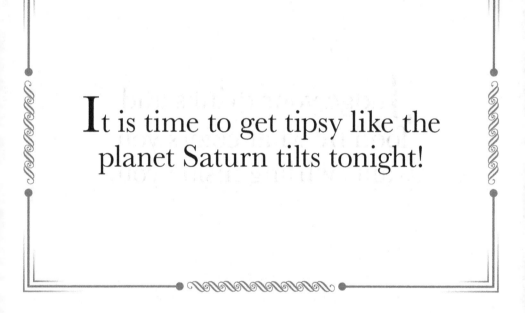

It is time to get tipsy like the planet Saturn tilts tonight!

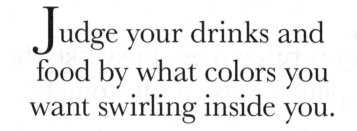

Judge your drinks and food by what colors you want swirling inside you.

Just like stars, all of us shine brightly.

Let God's creations be
your inspirations.

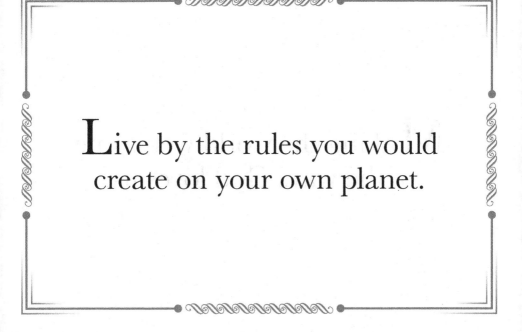

Live by the rules you would
create on your own planet.

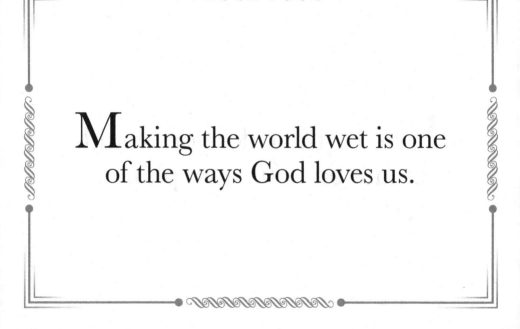

Making the world wet is one
of the ways God loves us.

Missiles might whiz around
you, yet continue your mission.

Mix touchable tools with untouchable thoughts, and then stir to get the best results.

Mold fantastic features
on your body.

Move megatons.

Organize your stuff like
God organized life.

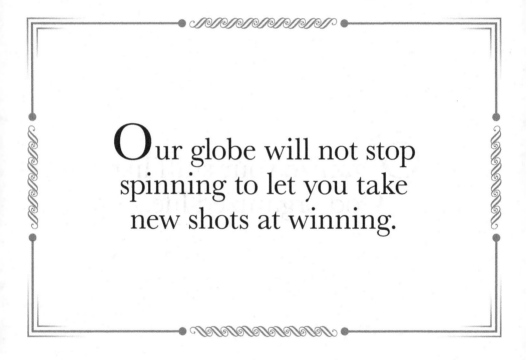

Our globe will not stop spinning to let you take new shots at winning.

Prove your love to
who you love.

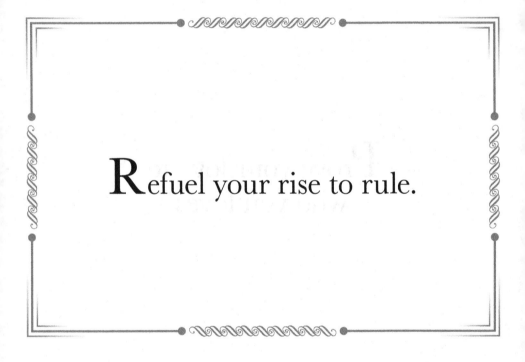

Refuel your rise to rule.

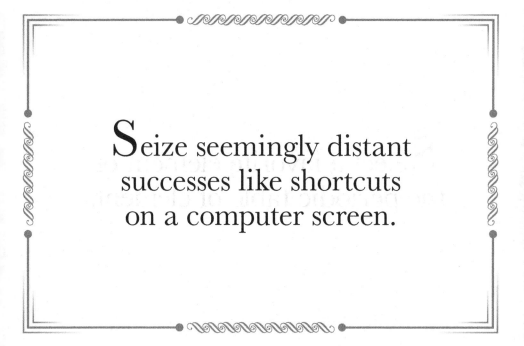

Seize seemingly distant
successes like shortcuts
on a computer screen.

Select a favorite element on the periodic table of elements.

Select one out of two
types of destinies that are
the good or the bad.

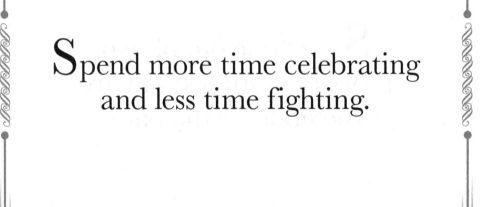

Spend more time celebrating
and less time fighting.

Stay on track on your trek in spite of the tricks of others.

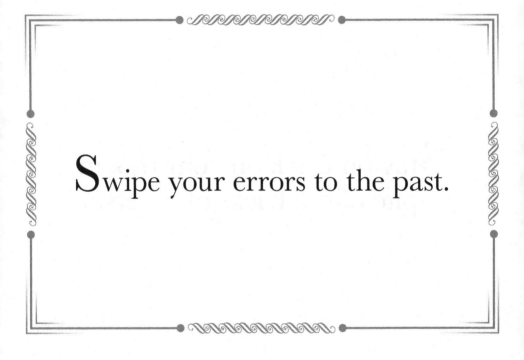

Swipe your errors to the past.

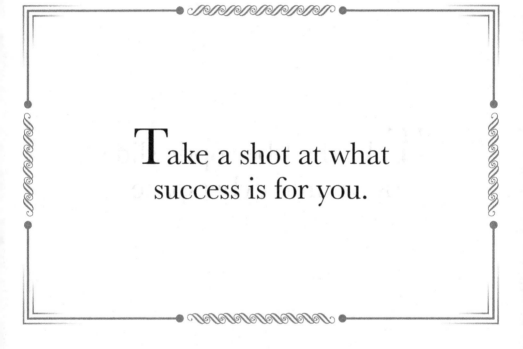

Take a shot at what
success is for you.

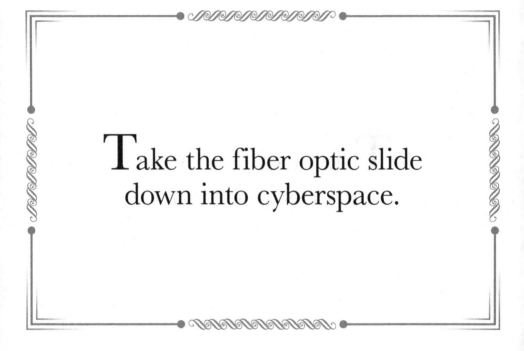

Take the fiber optic slide
down into cyberspace.

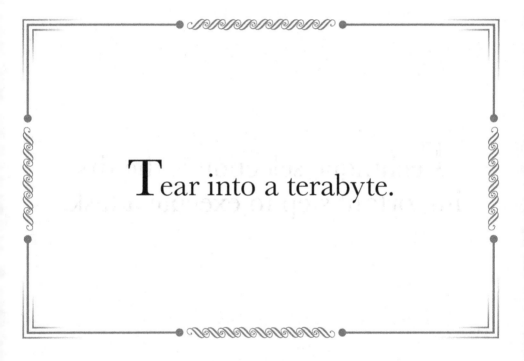

Tear into a terabyte.

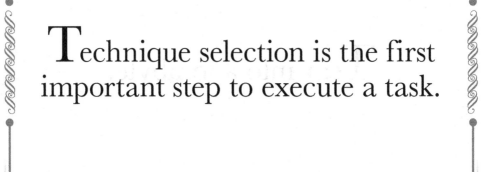

Technique selection is the first important step to execute a task.

The difference between good and evil is the good will try to win the battles longer and harder.

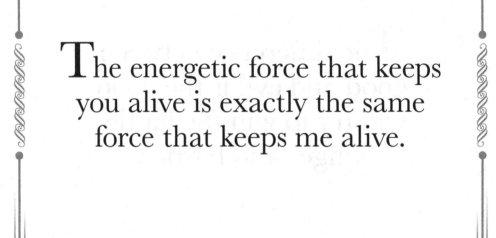

The energetic force that keeps you alive is exactly the same force that keeps me alive.

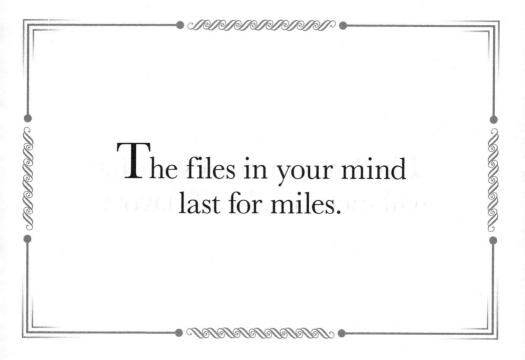

The files in your mind
last for miles.

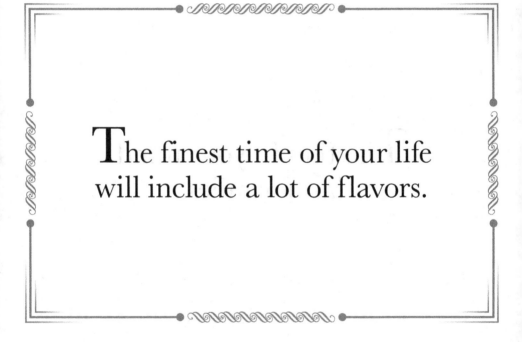

The finest time of your life
will include a lot of flavors.

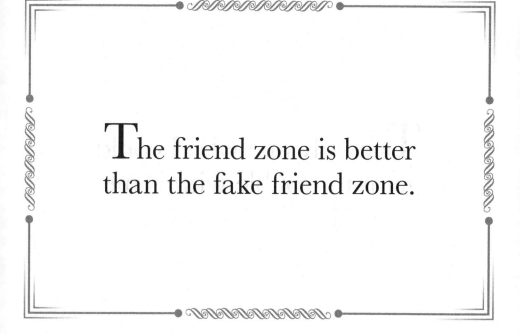

The friend zone is better than the fake friend zone.

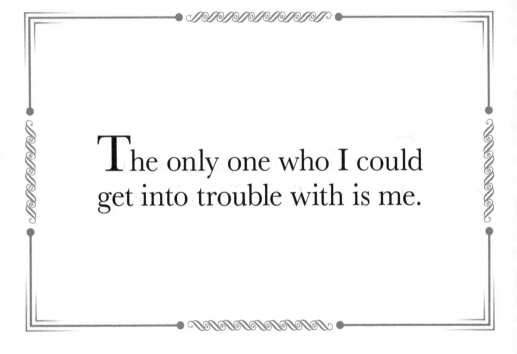

The only one who I could get into trouble with is me.

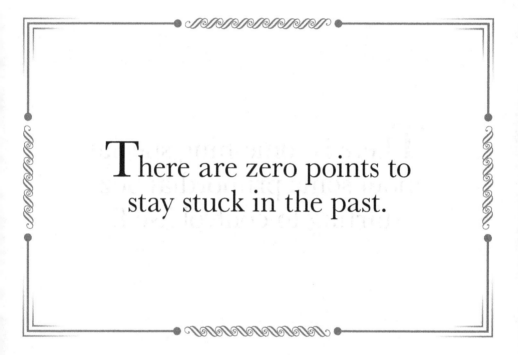

There are zero points to
stay stuck in the past.

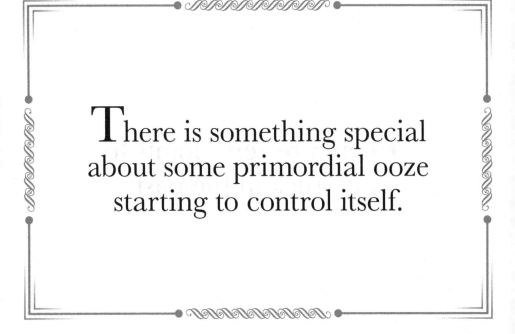

There is something special about some primordial ooze starting to control itself.

To forget the fun times
you had as a kid is bad
for your health too.

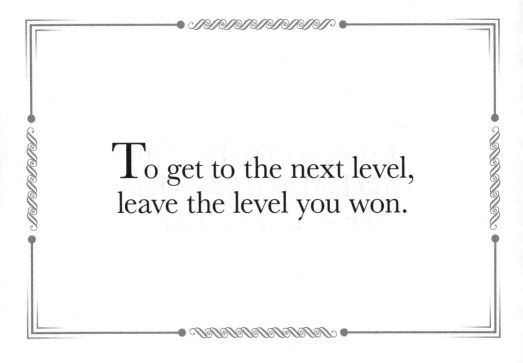

To get to the next level,
leave the level you won.

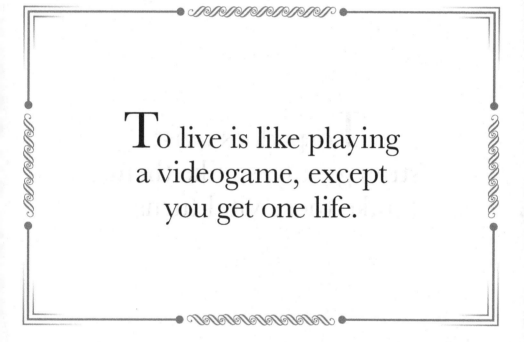

To live is like playing
a videogame, except
you get one life.

Torpedoes twist strategically, so like them, take those vital turns.

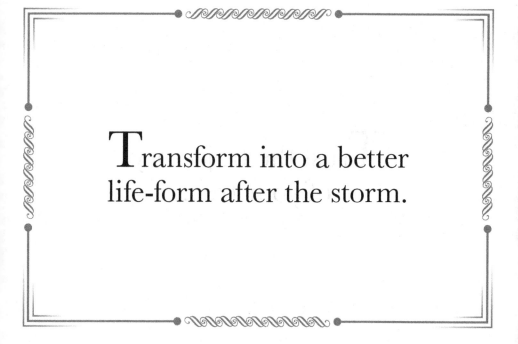

Transform into a better
life-form after the storm.

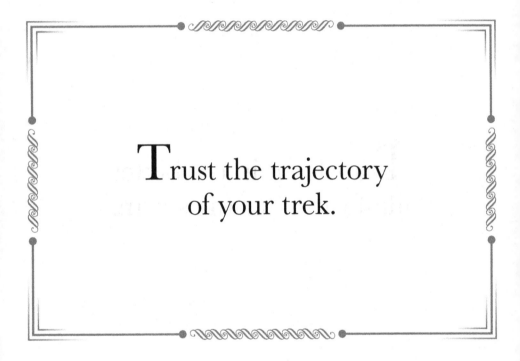

Trust the trajectory
of your trek.

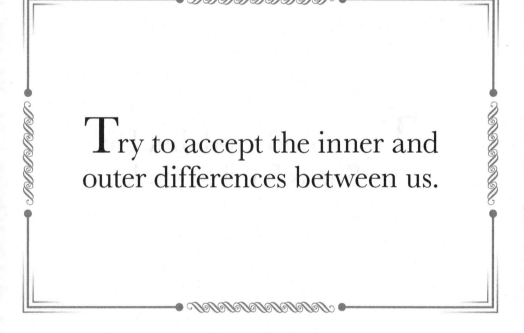

Try to accept the inner and outer differences between us.

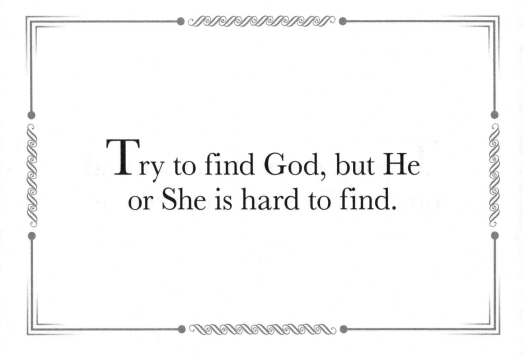

Try to find God, but He or She is hard to find.

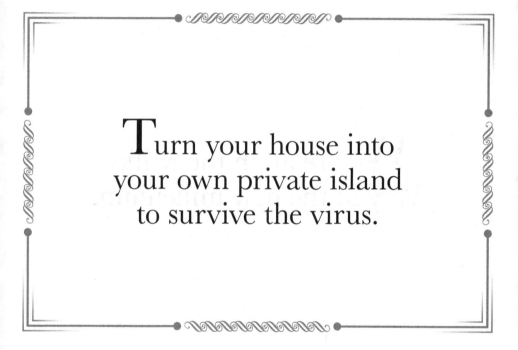

Turn your house into
your own private island
to survive the virus.

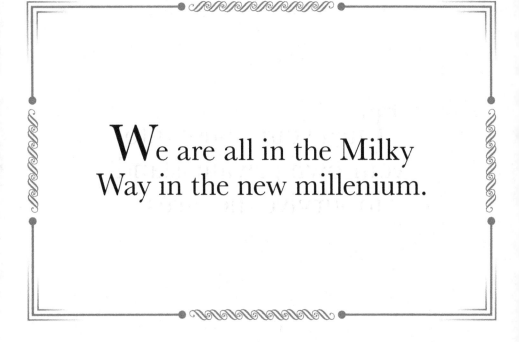

We are all in the Milky
Way in the new millenium.

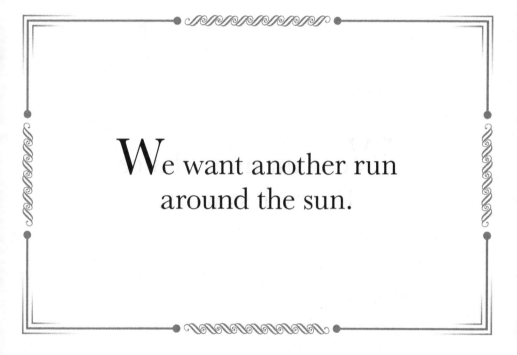

We want another run
around the sun.

We want more dance
floors, less wars.

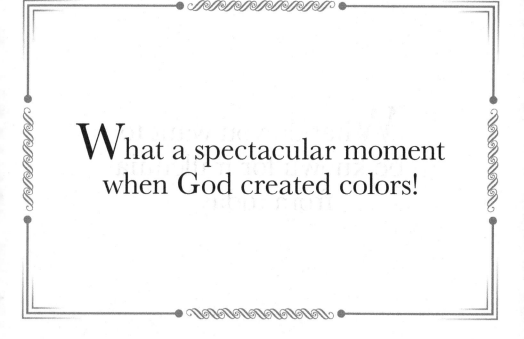

What a spectacular moment
when God created colors!

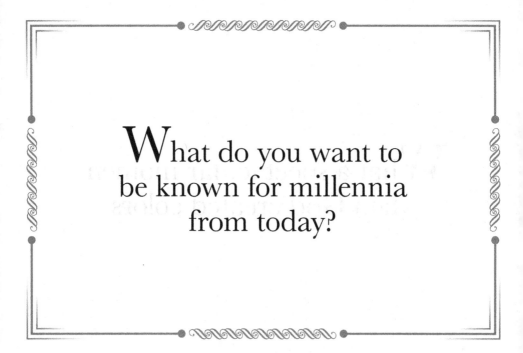

What do you want to
be known for millennia
from today?

What rules would you
create on your own planet?

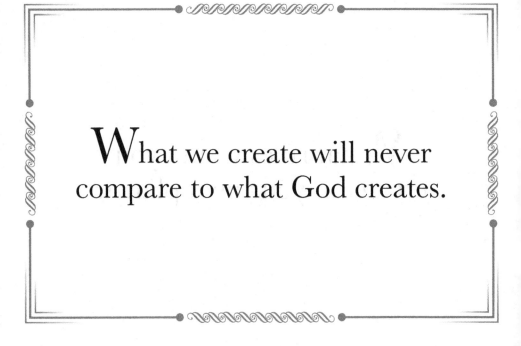

What we create will never
compare to what God creates.

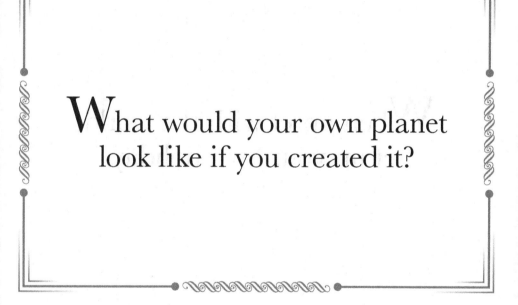

What would your own planet
look like if you created it?

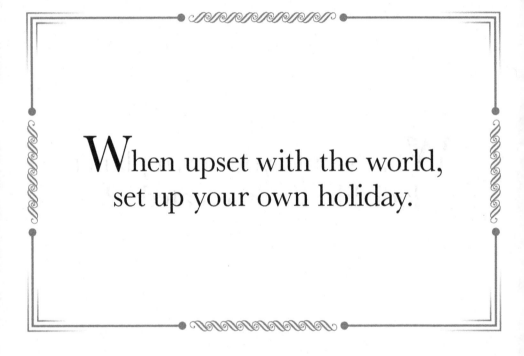

When upset with the world,
set up your own holiday.

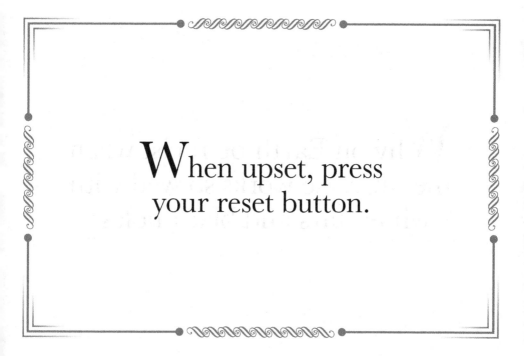

When upset, press
your reset button.

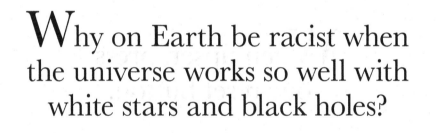

Why on Earth be racist when the universe works so well with white stars and black holes?

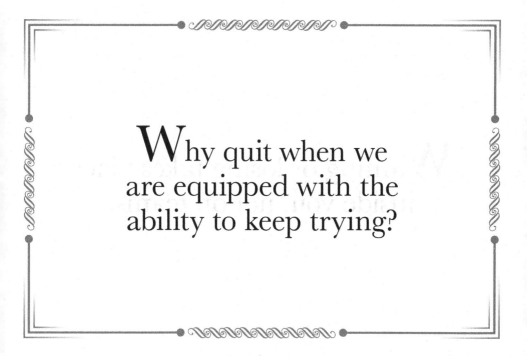

Why quit when we are equipped with the ability to keep trying?

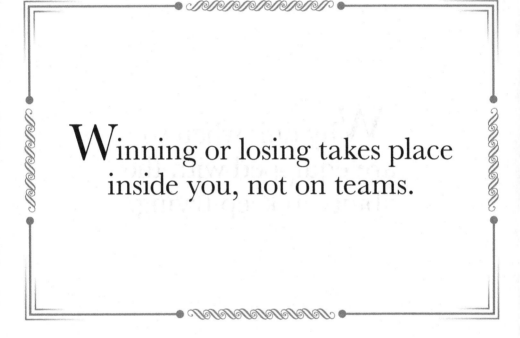

Winning or losing takes place inside you, not on teams.

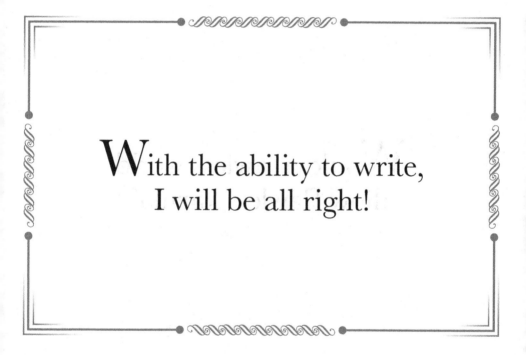

With the ability to write,
I will be all right!

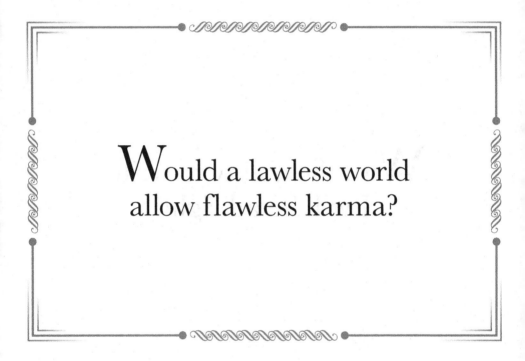

Would a lawless world
allow flawless karma?

You learn something new online every day.

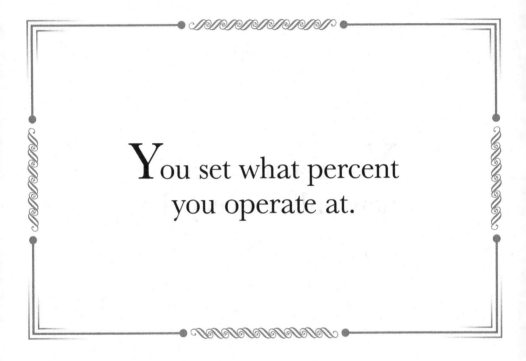

You set what percent
you operate at.

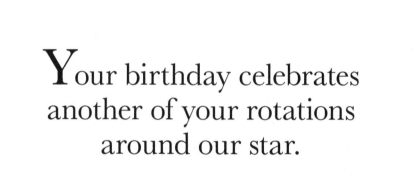

Your birthday celebrates another of your rotations around our star.

Printed in the United States
By Bookmasters